The Principle of Propriety

Story by: TAMEL LEE
Illustrated by: FLEANCE FORKUO

Published by Melanin Origins

PO Box 122123; Arlington, TX 76012

All rights reserved, including the right of reproduction in wholenor in part in any form.

Copyright 2022

First Edition

The author asserts the moral right under the Copyright, Designs and Patents Act of 1988 to be identified as the author of this work.

This novel is a work of fiction. The names, characters and incidents portrayed in the work, other than those clearly in the public domain, are of the author's imagination and are not to be construed as real. Any resemblance to actual persons, living or dead, events or localities, is entirely coincidental.

All rights reserved. No part of this publication may be reproduced, stored in a retrieval system or transmitted, in any form by any means without the prior consent of the author, nor be otherwise circulated in any form of binding or cover other than that with which it is published and without a similar condition being imposed on the subsequent purchaser.

Library of Congress Control Number: 2021942429

ISBN: 978-1-62676-065-3 hardback

ISBN: 978-1-62676-064-6 paperback

ISBN: 978-1-62676-063-9 ebook

The Principle of Propriety

"I will strive be correct in everything I do;
I will not allow others to influence me to do wrong."

www.MelaninOrigins.com

Marlon felt a bit sad about it, so he decided to send an email to the Mayor of Chicago in hopes that things could change for the better.

Marlon was surprised and excited at the same time, "Mayor Ausar!? I can't believe it's you! You really read my email?" Marlon asked.

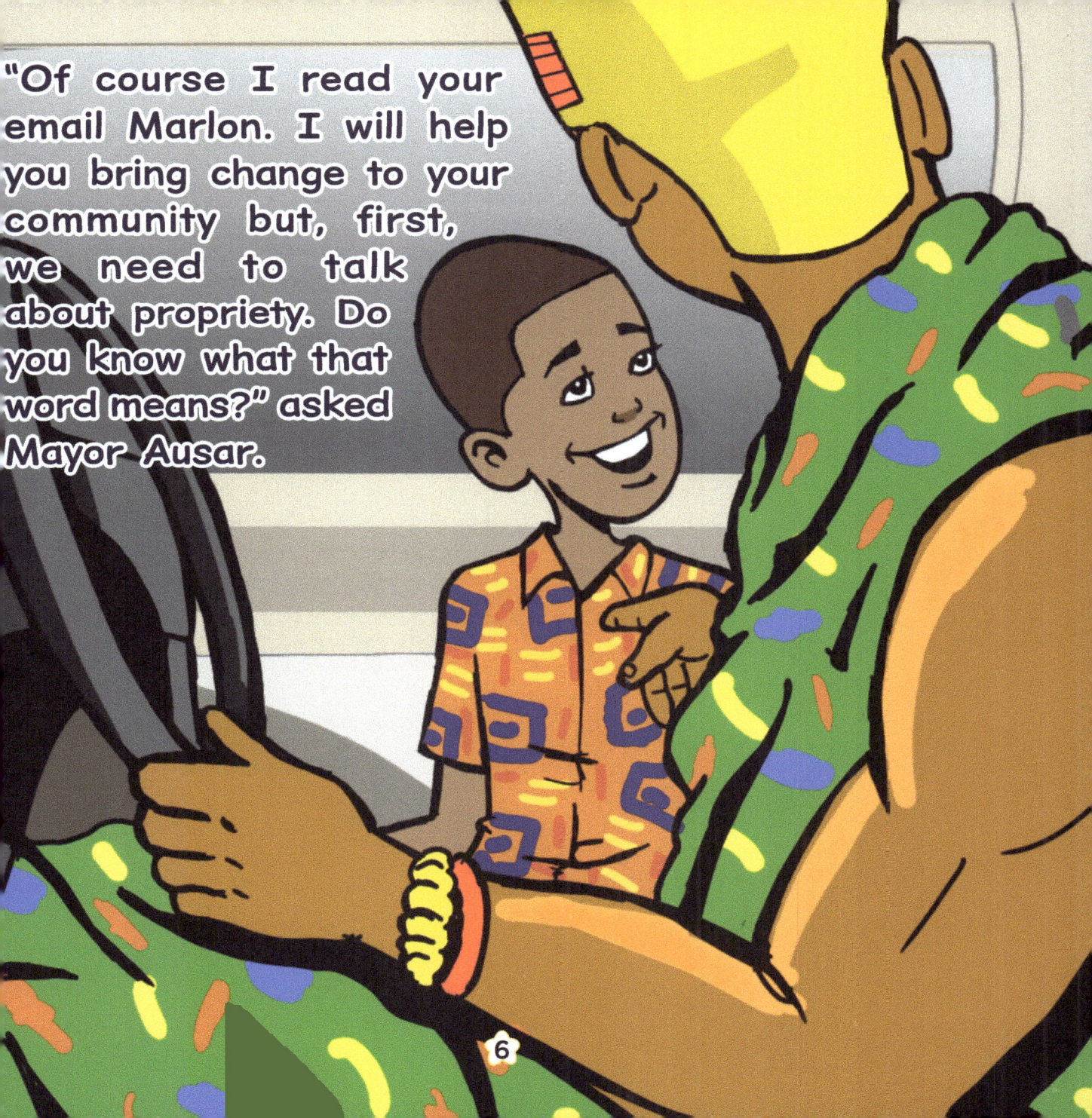

Mayor Ausar continued, "You're never too young to make a change in the community, Marlon. When we value propriety, we get a better understanding of what others are going through and how we can help them in meaningful ways."

Seven Principles of MA'AT

MA'AT is an ancient system of morals and values that guides thought and behavior in ancient Kemet (Egypt). It is also found in many other cultures in Africa.

1. TRUTH: based in fact with honesty and integrity.
2. JUSTICE: a state of fairness and lawful judgement.
3. RIGHTEOUSNESS: a state of consistent good conduct.
4. RECIPROCITY: "What goes around comes around"
5. BALANCE: an equal distribution of weight.
6. ORDER: everything in it's proper place and arrangement.
7. HARMONY: a pleasing arrangement of several elements all of one accord.

"The world is equally divided between good and evil. Your next act will tilt the scale" (African Proverb)

While enjoying a healthy meal, Marlon and Mayor Ausar shared ideas about the community center and had a great time getting to know each other.

The next day, Marlon showed propriety by respectfully knocking on doors, instead of banging on them, as he passed out his survey. He even picked up trash along the way.

Marlon explained how Mayor Ausar taught him to be a better leader by treating others with propriety, and he encouraged everyone to do the same.

Marlon learned that even though things may not always go the way we planned, we can always treat others with respect and take steps towards making a positive change in our lives and in our communities.

Modern Day Melanin Origins

This book is dedicated to Dr. Na'im Akbar, a true pioneer of our time.

Na'im Akbar, born on April 26, 1944 in Tallahassee, Florida, is a clinical psychologist, retired professor, publisher, and public speaker. Well known for his Afrocentric approach to psychology, he is a distinguished scholar and author of *Light from Ancient Africa and Know Thyself*. Many of his major works discuss mental health among African Americans.

Dr. Akbar is regarded by Essence Magazine as "one of the world's preeminent psychologists and a pioneer in the development of an African-centered approach in modern psychology." At Morehouse College, a Historically Black College/University in Atlanta, Georgia, Akbar designed and taught the first Black psychology course in the history of the college, and went on to develop the first Black psychology program there.

~ TheHistoryMakers.org

www.ingramcontent.com/pod-product-compliance
Lightning Source LLC
Chambersburg PA
CBHW040013080526
44586CB00028B/2995